Rocks and What We Know About Them

Geology for Kids

Children's Earth Sciences Books

BABY PROFESSOR

EDUCATION KIDS

Speedy Publishing LLC
40 E. Main St. #1156
Newark, DE 19711
www.speedypublishing.com

Rocks are everywhere on the surface of our Earth. Road-builders often have to cut through them to make the road flatter. Gardeners have to haul rocks out of the garden to make room for their plants. But what is a rock? What's it made of and where did it come from? Read on and find out!

Rocks make the skin of our Earth

The outermost layer of our Earth is called the crust. And the outermost layer of the crust is mostly made up of rocks. The whole Earth is about 4.5 billion years old and the oldest rock we have found so far is about four billion years old, so they've been here for a long time.

A rock occurs naturally in nature. It is a lump of minerals and solid crystals, tightly fused together by natural processes. On Earth there are three basic types of rock. These are igneous, sedimentary and metamorphic. Let's look at each type.

IGNEOUS ROCK

There's a lot of igneous rock on our Earth. Igneous rocks start as molten material in the Earth's mantle, the layer below the crust and form from volcanic action. Volcanoes bring igneous rock to the surface.

Igneous Rock

Igneous rock like granite forms when the molten material from the mantle rises up into the crust, but cools before it quite makes it to the surface. The outer core of our planet is about 95% igneous rock. To learn more about volcanoes, read the Baby Professor book, What Happens Before and After Volcanoes Erupt?

When the material that will become igneous rock is rising as magma, it is liquid. Its atoms and molecules mix together and then fuse into mineral grains as the magma cools and the rock starts to form. There are over 700 types of igneous rock.

Granite

Granite is at least 25% quartz. People use it often as a building material because it is so strong and durable. There's a lot of granite under the soil of every continent. Granite makes up a lot of the oldest rocks. However, when a piece of rock has been around for almost four billion years, it is sometimes a little hard to figure out what type of rock to call it!

Basalt

Under the seas the rock is mosly basalt, which is the most common rock that volcanic action creates. Basalt also makes up large parts of Hawaii, the midwestern United States and other places in the world where huge volcanoes spewed out large amounts of lava that flowed a long way before cooling into rock.

Pumice

Pumice is a very lightweight rock that sometimes forms during a volcanic eruption. If the conditions are right the molten rock when thrown into the air, form bubbles as it rapidly cools and loses pressure, turning into porous rock.

Pumice

Pumice may be relatively light, but it still does damage when it falls after being thrown into the sky by a volcano. When Mount Vesuvius erupted in Italy in 79 AD the eruption projected poisonous gases, masses of hot lava, ash and pumice stone into the air for a week.

The pumice and other material fell thickly on the ground, burying towns like Pompeii to a depth of several feet. Then rain melted the whole mess into a paste that hardened. The towns and the people who died in them, were buried from sight for almost two thousand years.

Obsidian

Obsidian is a form of volcanic glass. It forms quickly and has no crystal structure. Early humans formed tools and arrowheads out of obisidan when they could find it, making use of its sharp edges.

Tuff

Tuff is a fine-grained rock that forms from the ash volcanoes spew out.

SEDIMENTARY ROCK

Sedimentary rock forms from little bits of other rocks, from animal bones and even from parts of plants. The pieces can be as small as grains of sand.

The fragments build up in low-lying areas, like the bottoms of lakes or in valleys, over a long, long time. Then other layers of stuff build up on top of the lowest layers and the pressure of the stack compresses the lower layers until, gradually, they become solid.

You can often see the layers or strata, of material that built up to make sedimentary rock. The layers can be of different colors, reflecting the different mix of material in each layer. You can also find fossils in sedimentary rock!

When dinosaurs died often their bodies settled into the sand of a beach, a muddy shore or right down to the bottom of a lake. Then, as the sedimentary layers slowly built up and compressed, the bones of the dinosaurs would become preserved in the rock. The bones aren't made of bone material any more—they are more like a rock image of the dinosaur bones. There are different types of Sedimentary rocks.

Limestone

About 10% of sedimentary rock is limestone. It is mainly made up of tiny fragments of the skeletons of ocean creatures like coral, molluscs and forams. Chemically, it is mainly calcite and aragonite, crystal forms of calcium carbonate.

Sandstone

Sandstone is made of sand that has been compacted by intense pressure. The sand is small grains of rocks and some minerals like quarts and feldspar, which are the most common minerals in the crust of the Earth. Some sandstone holds up well against wind and weather and people use it for building or even to make walkways or roads.

Mudstone

Mudstone is at least one-third silt and one-third clay. Mudstone, sometimes called mudrock, accounts for more than half of the Earth's sedimentary rock. The elements that make up mudstone are so tiny that it is hard to study them without microscopes but sometimes the clay of a mudstone section may line up, making a visible streak.

Chalk

Chalk is a soft, white form of limestone. It is most famously on view along the White Cliffs of Dover, in southeast England.

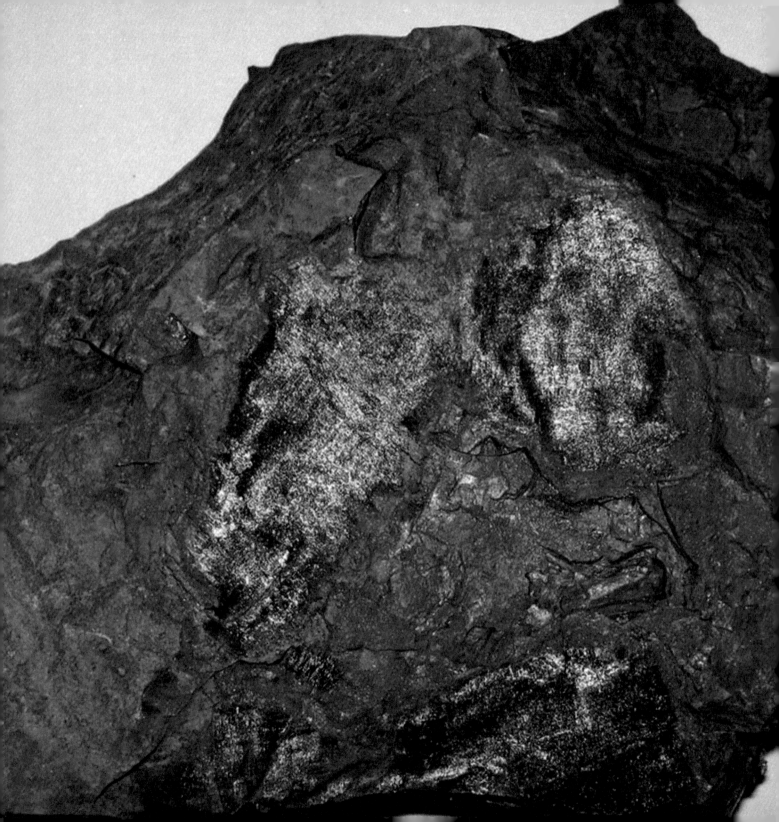

Coal

Coal is black or dark brown. It normally appears as a vein or seam among other layers of sedimentary rock. It is made of carbon and some other elements and forms when dead plant matter turns into rock.

The process involves the dead trees or other plants first becoming peat, then lignite, then sub-bituminous coal and bituminous coal. At the next stage, anthracite, coal moves over into the metamorphic rock category. The changes involve heat and pressure, and also biological processes and take place over a very long time.

Coal has been a major energy source throughout human history. Since it is created from plant matter and is largely carbon, it is a rock that burns! While coal is an important energy producer around the world, it also generates greenhouse gases and contributes to global warming and unhealthy air.

Flint

Flint is a hard crystal-like form of the mineral quartz. It usually appears as a mass or lump in chalk or limestone. Inside the mass flint can be gray, white, brown or green and often looks like glass or wax. People have used flint as a tool since the stone age since you can break off flakes of it and then work the flakes so they have and hold a sharp edge.

METAMORPHIC ROCK

Metamorphic rock starts as igneous or sedimentary rock. Then the Earth goes to work on it with heat and pressure or with naturally-occurring chemicals. The heat can come from hot springs or from magma nearby rising up toward a volcano or vent in the earth. The pressure can come from where two tectonic plates are pressing in to each other, making new mountains.

Metamorphic rock can get to the surface when a volcano spews it out or as part of the crumpling process when two tectonic plates collide. Both sedimentary and igneous rocks can become metamorphic rock.

From sedimentary rock:

- Marble starts out as limestone.
- Quartzite comes from sandstone.
- Slate begins as mudstone.

From igneous rock:

- Gneiss is often the result when granite is subjected to extreme heat and pressure.
- Granulite forms from basalt.

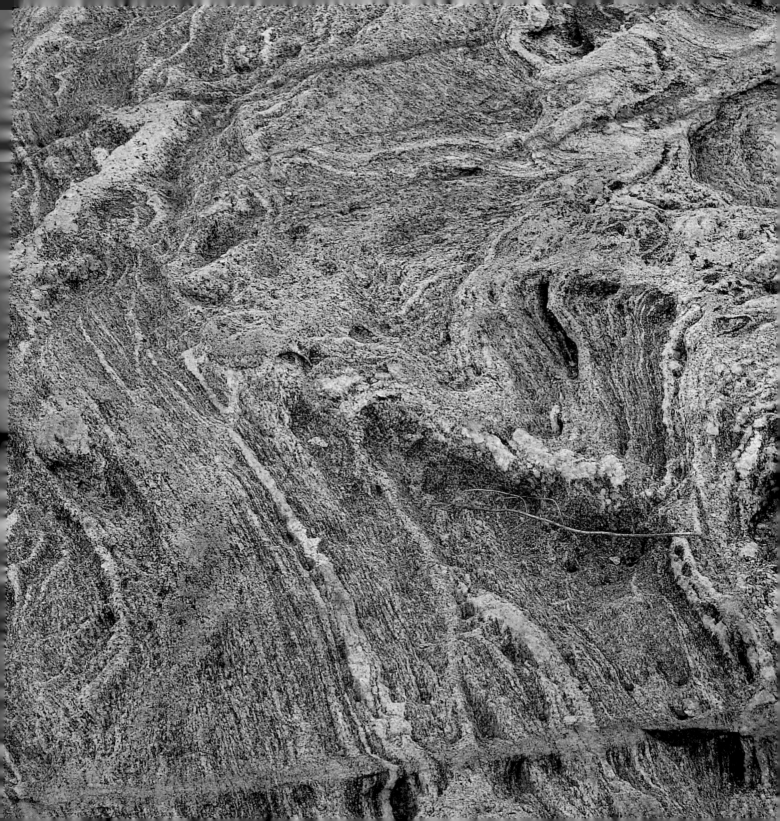

Humans and Rocks

Humans have used rocks ever since they started using anything! We have lived in caves in mountains or jumbles of large rocks. We have chipped flint and other workable rocks into edged tools and weapons and we have bound lumps of igneous rock to lumps of wood and used the result as clubs and hammers.

People have built small and huge houses out of rock, loosely piling the rocks up and holding them together with some sort of cement. They have also cut rock into blocks so carefully that the blocks fit together tightly and make a wall with no cement needed at all. People have set up rocks in circles like Stonehenge, perhaps for religious ceremonies and perhaps to study the sky and the seasons.

Amazing Earth

There's lots more to learn about the Earth beneath our feet. Take a look at Baby Professor books like Peeling the Earth like an Onion: Earth Composition to understand more about our planet.

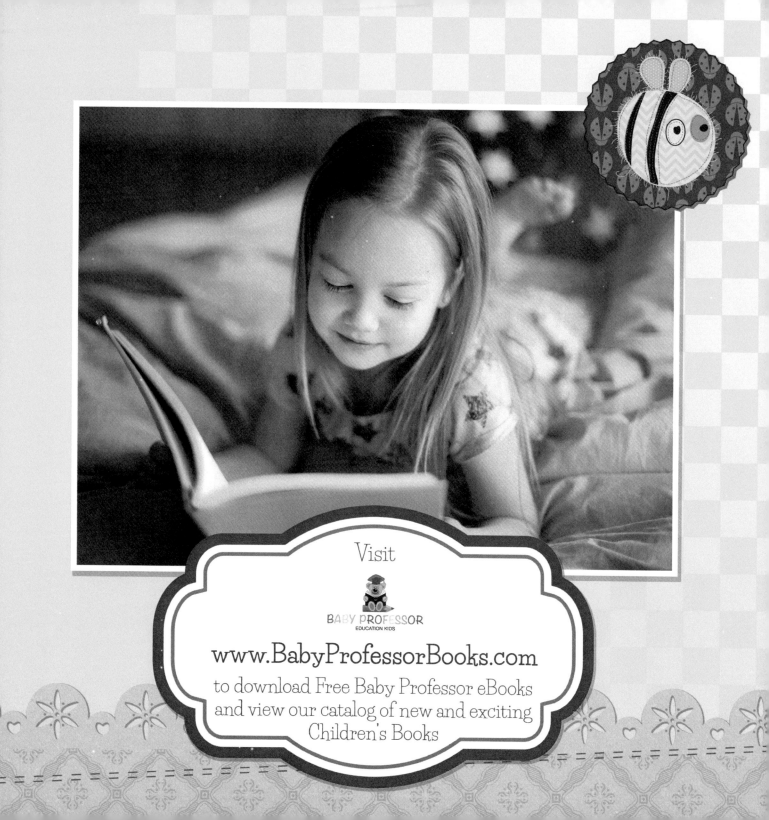